TWO-HEADED
NIGHTINGALE

New Issues Poetry & Prose

Editor   William Olsen

Guest Editor   Nancy Eimers

Managing Editor   Kimberly Kolbe

Layout Editor   Elizabyth A. Hiscox

Assistant Editor   Traci Brimhall

New Issues Poetry & Prose
The College of Arts and Sciences
Western Michigan University
Kalamazoo, MI 49008

First Edition, 2012.

ISBN-13   978-1-936970-07-0 (paperbound)

Library of Congress Cataloging-in-Publication Data:
Lessley, Shara
Two-Headed Nightingale/Shara Lessley
Library of Congress Control Number: 2011943422

Art Director   Ern Bernhardi
Designer   Lindsay Gilbert
Production Manager   Paul Sizer
                      The Design Center, Frostic School of Art
                      College of Fine Arts
                      Western Michigan University
Printing   McNaughton & Gunn, Inc.

TWO-HEADED NIGHTINGALE

SHARA LESSLEY

New Issues Press

<u>WESTERN MICHIGAN UNIVERSITY</u>

for my grandmothers
Carolyn Tomola and Jewell Gillam

Contents

Acknowledgments

Many thanks to the editors of the following journals in which these poems first appeared, sometimes in different versions:

Alaska Quarterly Review: "On the Subject of Want: The Sundew"
The Bellingham Review: "The Hydra"
Blackbird: "Wintering"
Black Warrior Review: "Intermission" (as "Intermission: *Roles for a Lifetime*")
Borderlands Texas Poetry: "Song for the Catatonic"
Clackamas Literary Review: "To My Father Two Years into Death"
The Cincinnati Review: "Photo of My Grandmother as Fieldworker, 1946"
Connotation Press: "Hopkins at the Window"
Crab Orchard Review: "Pomegranate"
Descant (Canada): "*Act I: The Master*," "*Act II: Costume Change*," "*Finale: Curtain Call*," "*Intermission*"
Fence: "Here Hangeth His Death in the Yard"
Gulf Coast: "Two-Headed Nightingale"
Hayden's Ferry Review: "Fallen Starling"
Isotope: "Self-Portrait as (Super/Sub) Pacific"
The Kenyon Review: "The Countervoice"
Meridian: "*Tooth of the Lion*"
Mid-American Review: "Canopy," "Genealogical Survey across Several Counties"
The Nation: "*The Firebird*"
New South: "This Way to the Egress"
Pleiades: "Captive," "Portrait *Hepialus*"
Ploughshares: "Field Song for Archey Valley in Her Mother's Mother-Tongue"
So to Speak: "Automata" (as "Self-Portrait as 18th Century Automata")

The Southeast Review: "After Reading Chu Shu-Chen, I Cube a
  D'Anjou"
Third Coast: "Blue Mussels," "Prometheus as Sparrow"
Threepenny Review: "The Peninsula"

"Tooth of the Lion" appeared in *Eco Poetry: A Contemporary
American Anthology* (Trinity University Press). "Two-Headed
Nightingale" was reprinted at *r.kv.r.y quarterly*. "Self-Portrait as
(Super/Sub) Pacific" received *Isotope*'s 2009 Editor's Prize for
Poetry.

For time, financial support, and community during the writing of
this book, I'm grateful to the Wallace Stegner Program at
Stanford University, the Olive B. O'Connor Fellowship at Colgate
University, the Reginald S. Tickner Fellowship at The Gilman
School, the Diane K. Middlebrook Fellowship in Poetry at the
Wisconsin Institute for Creative Writing, and University of
Maryland's MFA Program in Creative Writing. Many thanks to
the North Carolina Arts Council, Bread Loaf Writers' Conference,
Squaw Valley Community of Writers, The Writers' Colony at
Dairy Hollow (especially Marty and Elise Roenigk for providing
the Moondancer Fellowship in Nature and Outdoor Writing),
and "The Discovery"/*The Nation* Prize for additional fellowships,
scholarships, residencies, and awards.

For their criticism and generosity, I thank my teachers and
mentors: Elizabeth Arnold, Peter Balakian, Eavan Boland,
Michael Collier, W.S. Di Piero, Ken Fields, Michelle Mitchell-
Foust, Stanley Plumly, and Josh Weiner.

My sincere gratitude to the staff at New Issues, most especially
Nancy Eimers for her kindness and keen editorial suggestions.

For their enthusiastic support and feedback, I offer humble thanks to Robin Ekiss, David Roderick, Amaud Jamaul Johnson, Sara Michas-Martin, Rachel Richardson, Keith Ekiss, Brian Spears, Danielle Cadena Deulen, Jesse Lee Kercheval, Nick Lantz, John Rowell, Linda Trapp, Meg Tipper, and the members of the indefatigable "Anti-Workshop"—Katy Didden, Brian Moylan, and Alison Stine.

I am particularly indebted to Bruce Snider for his invaluable thoughts, insights, and enduring friendship.

Love and gratitude to my parents, Candi and Michael Tomola, for their years of good faith.

And to my husband, Kristian: thank you for being a trilogy.

I.

Split the Lark — and you'll find the Music —
—Emily Dickinson

Fallen Starling

Driven to land like light
it is unmade—or rather,
made into something other:

the bird so new its skull
tells its secret—bone-
cap clear as blown glass

through which one might trace
the almost-evolution
of faculties sewn in the little

sac of pigment. Body east;
head cocked west to expose
the undercarriage of beak,

the unguarded starling
becomes fodder for blackbirds.
Hard as nut or stone,

a monument eroding, its death
mask is a quilled machine,
odd series of belts and loops

burned into the sidewalk.
Stiff with sun, it is delicate:
the breast unstitched; freed,

the tiny heart. Unburdened,
the bird darts up its one good eye
to study its own undoing.

Captive

Locked inside my window,
        a cicada plodded above a death field

of insects: two bees, four flies,
        a dark basket resembling a spider. How it

got stuck there, I couldn't say,
        though as it clung to the ledge, then fell,

then mounted, I saw
        the wet-winged cicada wouldn't make it

without rescue. Claw clamped
        to the wire screen, it survived two days.

I even tried to set it free,
        forcing open the paint-sealed window

until it crashed swiftly down,
        sending me to the floor and the captive

back to its glass prison.
        I did mean to free it, sometimes pained

by its wings' screeching,
        pleading, but felt as if I could do nothing

in my despair; therefore,
        did nothing, no task a task I might accomplish.

I let it die, and it felt
        good to let it. The death, proof of my consequence,

or that I might be
capable of love, if only to withhold it.

The Peninsula

And when autumn finally arrived, I drove
to the southernmost point of Maryland—
strip of land like an outstretched arm
holding a lighthouse in its palm, tower's

> base weathered by surge, half ocean,
> half Potomac. And when sundown came

and the tourists had gone, I walked the jetty,
as we too had walked, plotting from rock
to rock, until we reached the crest, then rested,
our bodies towering over granite.

> From boat or car, we could've been
> any two people watching the bay

merge with something greater: blue-brown
river joining the sea, orange canker
festering in the leaves and brush behind us.
And when your words returned, I found

> a few yards from shore, the place
> soldiers built a hospital to house the Rebel

wounded. Pointing to a stack of planks
you traced the moat and mapped the perimeter,
though "no sane man" would swim to war,
but wait it out for his body to heal, or

> the tide to turn, so he too might
> return home, worn as a field

torn open by rain—which is really
the earth being broken, or the sound we make
breaking each other in silence,
something turning the air—a coldness

      neither can explain but senses
      massing gradually toward us.

Portrait *Hepialus*

the *ghost moth*

Shivering nightmare gleaming like light,
        you tap and hiss as the dead do nightly.

Not content to idle in trees, nor to
        unthread nectar from orchids, you survive

on a diet of tears, fanning out below
        the dark, clouded pool in the cow's eye,

your wings shuddering like a pair of lashes
        batting back the sun. Your ghosts revisit

every season: feeding on evening
        primrose or piercing summer's seeded grape;

burrowing into the heart of winter
        legumes, causing dried beans to twirl

and skip through air as if possessed.
        Fat and yellow as pollen sacs, you feast

on fall; by spring, spin yourself
        an ash overcoat to mourn the flower-

like catkins of elm. Remarkable
        your appetite, your power to transform,

your benisons: bravery, renewal.
        That you bore into coffins—drilling

through century-old oak, rustling, fluttering,
        haunting the skulls of kings—then emerge,

racing sightless through night in pursuit
       of a lover, your flared wings patrolling

her scent: part defense, part desire.

Blue Mussels

Of how to begin to collect them,
    to patiently clip the fringe binding
        each valve together, I know little.

And of what it takes to scrape
    the casings of seaweed and grit. I know
        only they are to ocean what grass is

to stretches of prairie and meadow,
    that is, a piece of something entire,
        and when steamed in wine or water,

what they mean to you. So tonight
    as you fork out the meat, blue mussel
        unhinged, I feel I understand why

one divides in two. Ancient husk.
    Pale tongue a salt-lick pressed
        by restrictions that shape it.

If I could pry you open. Pluck you
    from your watery nest. If I could close
        myself inside your airtight chamber,

bed down on your living flesh.
    If the softest part of ourselves
        wasn't hidden, what of earth or light

might we remember? What speck
    of dust would we recall? Back and forth,
        back and forth. A near invitation.

Only now does the alabaster dish
       seem to me two's division: empty shells
         words we've so often rehearsed

and worn the human out of.

On the Subject of Want: The Sundew

Phosphorus in short supply, a damsel-
fly's no better than a dung midge or gall:

shiver of wing and the tentacle seizes—
each kiss an acidic whip-stitch needling

the gnat deeper in basal rosette. Condemned
carnivorous, boggy assassin—I say

we've much to learn from you, ruby.
What's beauty, really, to do with lust?

Leave pearly-eyed pipevines their minute
to mate in chalky stalks of moss;

bedding in sludge, let northern emeralds
divide the seconds. Save, instead, this

night coaxed into the next—black
remains of inedible leg dismantled

then spat back for days—your sticky
fists reluctant to unclutch what's

wanted, your leaves so pungent with glue,
touched once, no lover can return to.

Wintering

Already, winter makes a corpse of things.
Snow reshapes what frost has taken. You've lost

interest in letters. So let sunrise come.
Let smoke grow darker by the light of day—

what I could spare of you I've burned already.
The fencepost needs repair. Let sunrise come.

Let panels of light make thirsty the ice-
caked stump of oak. Let the sky go empty

as December's intimations, when in snow
we fashioned ourselves side by side as fallen

angels: yours, the greater wingspan; my outline
barely reaching. Daybreak. I lay my body down

in powder. Roots torque up through the chest's
blankness, snarl of knots unloosed. *What comes,*

on parting you insisted, *will come.* Ice splits,
in the distance. What breaks will break. Let it.

II.

Two-Headed Nightingale

Christine & Millie McCoy, 1851–1912

tear open the breast   and heart to tell
    biological truth: no: the black, deformed
    birth: yes: slavery   of the interior

unlock the shackled   spine to show
    in sixty-one years   monstrosity: yes:
    she never left my side   the fusion of vertebrae

the malformation   of blood and bone
    collision? no   *our walk, a side-step*
    the backbone braided   *dance: a waltz*

born 1851   as slaves: the body
    twice betrayed: *the sky*   *held the sun: no, moon*
    "MOON AND SUN   UNITED ON STAGE"

illusion? no: *miracle*:   the sisters
    merged, their voices   layered like the nightingale's
    sheath of feathers,   light hitting its wings

breaking up light—   *negress?* no: they are
    crimson blazing,   their song quick and agile
    as their hearts' pumping: yes: one beat:

one pulse: *one soul, two*   *thoughts*, from darkness,
    a final note   dividing the air: the sudden
    breath rushing to fill   the other's departure

The Old Life

> *A person's body first has to learn to sing in silence*
> —Gelsey Kirkland

ACT I: The Master

His ballets were his—

that much was clear
even when *count six*
meant *hold eight*

third was *first*
and *Take five!* went

ten-fifteen-twenty
is he ever *coming*
back? We agreed
three days in, I'd been

mis-cast. He screamed;
I turned. He beat

the floor; I leapt.
Higher he moaned
stupid girl! Stupid

stupid girl! I rolled
off pointe, said

nothing. Every night,
the corps let out
early; I stayed,
last to gather my things,

last to wind the theater,
heat of lights, of stage—

he'd asked me to stay,
            he'd asked me
to stay

pressed to the wall,
his hands

roaming; still
I held, thinking *move, move*

move stupid girl.

Intermission

I never played with dolls. *Coppélia* is a doll;
Swanilda poses as a life-size doll to win
the affections of *Franz*, lost in the opening act.

Female teachers are mistresses; men, masters.
I made a career of mastering the *Mad Scene*.
Forget what's meant for show: my *Giselle*

danced herself to death on stage,
offstage. Is there a difference? *Arabian*
caged me as an exotic peacock locked

in a wheel-away cup steamed with dry ice,
allergic. If only the audience knew
I hate *Coffee*. I hate *Snow*. Playing in it;

playing it. Try waltzing over bobby-pins,
rosin, lost sequins and swept-up dust from god-
knows-how-many-shows. By cue, the soft

flakes begin to fall and with them, every bit of
what's been swept for weeks by techies
between Acts I and II. The stage is a death trap.

We were taught as girls when looking in
the mirror to see *Kitri*, source of lust; *Odile /*
poor drowned *Odette*; *Juliet*, the child bride;

commendable *Clara* who slays the *Mouse King*.
We were offered surgeries to break our arches;
rivals to watch our weight. In exchange

for our bodies, we were presented roles
for a lifetime. How, then, could I so long
have missed it? *Medora* is sold at auction;

La Sylphide loses her wings. A woman is
not a swan. Still I stood backstage, plotting
darkness night after night, watching

The Ballerina kill *Petrouchka* with her coldness,
my heart racing, waiting for my turn.

ACT II: Costume Change

That weekend, flames seized the black hills
surrounding our tour-stop: creeping down

the ledge near Turtle Rock, thirteen fires
across a 160-mile radius. In air: a cindered

stench. Exhaust. Scorched eucalyptus.
Bits of soot rising through the floor vents.

Per our instructions, the cast stayed put.
I slept, then dressed for morning class,

trudging up the rolling hillocks toward
the studio, my hair, drizzled with leaden

snow that fell from the trees—eerily
silent. Full barre. For forty-five minutes

we wheezed through warm-up before
heading center, working the usual positions.

From petite to grande allegro, I pitched
my tired weight in air—*again, again* faster

again—until, SNAP! the ankle's outer tendon
sent a sharp rush of heat up the Achilles,

whose clipped strings jerked me, shrieking,
to the floor where they found me: dark

bird—that for all its practice—could not
lift itself, somehow back out of the ashes.

Finale: Curtain Call

bone spur. ice. class. audition. height: training: weight: 103. cast. rehearsal. sweat. bone spur. master. shave. bone spur. hunger. pianist. *Pas de Quatre.* bone spur. tendonitis. class. class. rehearsal. hunger. opening night. backstage. downstage. (*upstaged?*) bone spur: Larkspur; next stop: Somewhere, Arizona. matinee. master. conductor. doctor. *Bluebird. Firebird.* swelling. waltz. Vaganova. Petipa. Balanchine. Choo San Goh. class. class. cattle call. contract. costume fitting. hunger. moleskin. thick skin. pressure. performance. notes. paycheck. bobby-pin. bobby-pin. understudy (paranoia). ice. heat. snow. sweat. rest. bus. bruising. ice. heat. pills. hunger. Psoas. socket. inflammation. turn-out. turn-*out!* *ronde de jambe en l'air.* center. crutches. callback. corps. insurance? paycheck. lights. fever: 98. hunger. sternum. pelvis. weight: 96. act three: bruising. nail-bed. surgery. sidelines. ice. rest. return. elevation. class. promotion. cast: *Giselle*
mirrors. safety-
pin.   clippers.   costume.   premiere.
Places!
backstage   hunger
numbness   *bone-*
spur-bone-loss-tendonitis-clicking-hip medics
make-up   tulle garland
entrance:
Mad Scene
Mad Scene

black-out
curtain

applause

Automata

On my inverted marriage-bed the bride-
    groom bleeds, somewhere beyond this
        rectangular frame, these gilded walls

the artisan's whittled from love to cage me.
    My maker sees no shame in it: rigged
        breasts heaved by wire strings; my eyelids

like theatrical backdrops that fall and lift
    via pulley. Evenings, he winds the key;
        in ecstasy, an asp entwines my feet,

its double rising by musical cue toward
    my wrist, glistening mother-of-pearl.
        I am childless. Only voles and field-

mice latched in corners catch my
    beauty's deformity: oversized eyes
        animated as three chords peak,

and the great snake strikes, my body
    writhing and writhing without me,
        my mouth strained open

till the lark is just a sullen mound of
    feathers, whose rustling has ceased,
        and from my limbs, my lovers slink

back up the bed-posts' trunks, where, coiled
    in the canopy's branches, their mechanical
        shadows have no living sources in the trees.

The Firebird

Ballets Russes: *Tamara Karsavina, June 1910*

Breast
    thrust frontward,
    her pointe-work's *one-three-two one-two* proves
    (pride, fear, pleading, might) more
to flight than either feather or

wing.
    Everything
    about this bird is built for likeness—
    beveled tail arched back, she
razes the air about her. Even

the
    huntsman burns:
    plucking her coxcomb, the fire-dazzled
    image singed in his noble
glove. Of bodice, plumage, costume,

crown,
    only her
    ruin seems human—yes, hers is that
    old tale in a nutshell:
the egg contains the soul. Threatened,

her
    delicate
    honeycombed bones wrench back to divert
    the magician king. Love's
ultimate sacrifice! Art,

33

none-
      theless, knows
   too the meaning of stillness: so holds
      the bird her final pose
as her prince (with his mistress) departs—

though
      who, when pressed
   to detect on that darkened stage even
      the slightest quiver, could
fail to recognize the remark-

able quickness of her caged-in heart?

Song for the Catatonic

1950: she spent two years carving her self-portrait before doctors
released her

Because the tree became her—
    fallen among the upright. Because the apple wood
        split in two. Because its rawness drew her,

in un-reason they saw reason.
    Because the knotted waist twisted like intestines,
        tangled blight dividing the trunk and branches

like the illness that addled
    her mind. Through cinnamon and rot she hacked—
        shaving the wood, slashing the chest (like hers)

cratered with tuberculosis.
    Her making marked progress. It pleased them:
        this rigidity, this transformation, the pair of arms

fixed in the perfect expression
    of self-restraint, incapable of harm.
        Tear the mouthless face! Tear the incapable-of-

breathing-seeing-saying-face!
    She whittled as they watched; became the tree
        when they didn't. She coaxed music from branches—

the long-held notes and sudden
    staccato rising and falling like the unsteady
        score of thought. They found it beautiful

because she carved from sickness
a body to house her mind. She worked till
there was nothing. Nothing.

III.

The Countervoice

Yourself, the rule.
Yourself the maker of its exception.
Snow fills the nest's ladle.

Whiteness. Talons clasped,
the cardinal sits on the ice-
clipped bough, motionless. Everything

bleached to nothing. The bird's
undistracted color: winter's counterpoint.
Should survival require such deliberate

action? That difficult
grace called once
in defense, not too unlike a bird

fallen less from flight
than instinct. What I wanted was
to know what sadness isn't

in part exhaustion?
Something ravenous not ravenous
enough. Unattended to, the nest

naturally spills over; self-
induced or by accident, the heart
just stops. Like silence: snow drifting,

drifting. Often I thought,
if only I could make myself
still enough. Porcelain still. Cardinal

still. Go farther even,
inside. *This too shall pass,*
                    I reasoned, not knowing

what (if anything)
to answer. Not knowing then, too
                    often a bird will not abandon

the branch that snaps beneath it.

Field Song for Archey Valley in Her Mother's Mother-Tongue

In times of survival, there are no decisions

       great or small—as a girl, my grandmother killed

a copperhead with a broomstick,
beating its pitted skull until her father's dirt-damp

floor shined bright as a penny. There was

no money. The traps went empty. Listen:
       my grandmother's mother dies of *pellagra*—

       *

diarrhea / deficiency / dermatitis /

       dementia. Pre-Depression: there's little red

meat to be found, but scraps of pork-fat, scant molasses and corn-
meal. Children creep out from the hills

       boosting each other up through the window to

witness Eula Belle—"that half-wit"—pick and eat

       *

her scabs. My grandmother's seven;
drives them all back with a mule-switch. His wife

       hauled off like an auctioned hog, a husband will often turn

on his daughter before taking a second bride. 1925:

the siblings number sixteen (grandma's age, and the year
she will marry)—his and hers and theirs. Soon, her stepmother loses

    interest, drawing ("just enough") water each morning to wash

her tar-black hair. A drought comes;

    *

the pump begins to rust. Second verse: the family has

    few options. In an eastern hamlet

near the convergence of Hartsuggs Creek
hunger rattles the one-room shack
    while, thigh-deep in a chigger-

infested field, a girl chafes clean each cell
of the knocked-loose hive, taking

    welts with honey. Against dying

    *

light, she dips in the end of an inflamed
finger she'll later

coax her infant

    sister to suckle the tip of, as if such

flesh were her mother's own dark nipple, returning amber-
rose in the wet shade of Arkansas

dusk that burns and glistens like some rare

unpolished stone.

Metronome

In the long night called girlhood the heart holds
tight in its bony crate. Like a bird of fire caged.
Its throat repeats *two notes two notes* as light steals
into its open beak the slightest bit of feeling. Yet

plains trembling under Wyoming sun cannot coax it,
nor eucalyptus seething along the Pacific coast;
not the gulf's drinking hole, the desert's vaulted dome.
The sky's gaping invitation has clipped its wings.

But isn't the kept bird most beautiful, like isinglass?
On its swing beneath the windowsill the red wings
pulsing like a timepiece that, suspended from a string,
catches light, casting shadows across the bed sheets.

Genealogical Survey across Several Counties

My inheritance is a thumbnail's splinter;
a pocket lined with grease. I come

from a frayed line, DNA's loose
stitch—on my mother's side: five

suicides, a history of heart disease and cancer
wards. My father's bankrupt mother mourned

four husbands. Outside Edmond, Oklahoma,
mother's mother buried twins in a shoe-box.

I come from a thin line tacked with spotted
muumuus, cloth diapers patched and re-worn

a dozen times over. My grandfather couldn't tread
the sidewalk straight, so shot himself

in front of his children. My father fell
to his death; men chalked his likeness half

past West Street. I come from a line wrapped
round the courthouse, from papers filed

for persons missing. I'm left guessing
my great-grandmother's passing, but carry

her name in my wallet. Each decade the letters
grow faint as a paper fortune

dissolved in the wash. I never could sew
by the numbers—fabric of being, a clumped

sequence of pinpricks and knots. Needle
plunged in the finger's tip, a constellation

spilled across linen—how the stars
leak out. One September, I pierced my ears

with my uncle's hook and fish-line, sour
lobes milky with infection. Static

in the phone-line, I couldn't hear
my father's censure. Lightning that night

I sat on his lap, driving out in the country.
Everything cold and wet. Cords of rain

erased the wiper's blade. A fine line
as we chased the storm, a slim partition

holding disaster back. I could barely see
past the wheel. Follow the lines, he said, meaning

the tar-slick break between asphalt
and field? At the fork, a county marker

appeared at last, and the earth opened, raw
as the sun pushed up—a sign,

he told me, we'd finally crossed over.

Having It Out with God

If prayer begins in darkness, then this:
waiting it out among the little live things

taking shelter in an abandoned barn,
their nests built from threads filched

from canvas feed bags. The moon is
unforgiving, radium-glow singeing

my thin skin. Night's eye holds me
in its dull stare. If there is a God, I doubt

I have the heart to bear it. Quick flash
darting over the belly-crawl of bramble:

a camp of bats surges from the open
mouth of sky. Through the rafters,

my flashlight shifts; bait and switch, until
I find it—membrane of tail and wing

roosting singly, tucked grayish-brown
into itself, as if the others' ultra-

sonic call were above its range of hearing,
as if, though sleeping soundly

through the cold, it might one day
reawaken to open its clasped hand.

Hopkins at the Window

Past darkness he pitches bits of plaster.
Bats wobble and dart. *My eyes are small
and dull,* he writes an artist friend, *of
a greenish brown; hazel I suppose.* Grey-
gold, the suicide's own eyes put out
with a wire and stick in a nettled field—
he's seen the boy at mass—a medical
apprentice, he later learns, who likewise
liked to paint. *In mind or body or both,
I too shall give away.* Then, in a dream
his body does give way, or his mind
as the crucified hand he sketches
reaches toward him; he wakes
aroused. A gas-lamp flickers across
the chamber pot, his wall's moldy
rings. The stacks of exams he knows
are enough to carry him to spring.
Christ's work, his director assures,
such tests. Of his annual lectures
a student remembers best
not some theory of divinity nor sixth
form's elegiac storm, but the afternoon
when pressed for his Latin cribs
how he confessed to a toothache instead;
and how the excitable Hopkins dashed
from the room and bade the boy to follow—
out of the building, across the yard
where the priest climbed twenty feet
up a rain-slick football post
above St. Stephen's green. *Pain's remedy
is prayer,* he exclaimed, tight-walking
the iron stretch between the poles,
or distraction. Now tell me how do you feel?

Yet, there are aches Hopkins knows
that are too real. *I never saw a woman
nude*, he tells a class. And glancing
from his text, *I wish I had*. It's hills
he sees instead, and the *beak-leaved
boughs* he sketches in a letter as trees
outside his window scrape and wheeze
in darkening forms. His December's
almost worn. *My Father, my God—*
the daily breviaries past. Gnats circle
and flit toward the glass. The sky turns
wet and mild. A faint rasping
in his chest: *how long does the sun have left?*

Tooth of the Lion

Not footsteps-of-spring or devil's lettuce. Not
hound's tongue, Spanish lotus, Spanish broom.
Not the hottentot fig, its acrid center an unripe

lemon pared in two. Not vanilla leaf, nor bitterroot.
Not the five-fingered fern, glove of spinach
palm faced up, as if about to be read its fortune.

Not creeping snow-berry. Not the hairy fringepod
whose leaves hang down like hand-carved paper
ornaments. Not even the hot-mouthed venus

thistle or scarlet pimpernel compare. Look past
the coastal orchids' loose flirtation, the poppies'
turned-up cheeks. Past the sunflower and tom-cat

clover. To know what it is to stand alone
face into the wind, it's *dent-de-lion*—it's what is
least desired. Sour stem of milk. Erratic growth.

The globular seedball identified as burden. Shelter
for the black beetle, grasshopper, garden centipede.
Fodder for goldfinch and honeybee. Lightweight

crown of bristle broken once to braid a necklace,
chain, or held to the lips to predict a future
which seemed then, so far off. The dandelion's

core dispersed to places unimagined. Chorus
of a hundred directions. Each sliver
a possibility somewhere anchoring itself in dirt.

Photo of My Grandmother as Fieldworker, 1946

Up to her elbows in horseflies, chiggers
whipping their forked tails,

        her good years muddied

in other peoples' crops: she did

what she had to, picking
through aphids,

parasitic clusters. And this,
        I get, is the trick of it: "making

do," waist-deep in frost-
bitten cotton

        whose thorny bolls will scar
      the hands that cannot

not feed her children, dragging

a bag—that weighs

        more than a man—behind her,

while my mother stirs
so deep in her pelvic bowl it feels

like the dark

      pangs of hunger rolling again
in waves. And the milky

stalk triggered in her breasts'
damp bed? She thinks, *just a salty*

band of sweat, another stain

to scrub from her husband's second-
hand britches whose buttons,

      reflected against the foreman's

watch, shine

         bright as metal stars—

Neither Falling Nor Rising

The wasp performs against a nectarine
a daughter's lonely sentence, its blunt

head charging that which it can't swallow.
Is a word a covenant? A child,

I watched her callused hands force fields
in the grammar of nectar and bloom.

Roots transformed into something useful.
How I wanted to be *butter pear*, or that knotted

bruise *persimmon*. Unlike the bee, a solitary
wasp is parasitic: its nest, shaped from

paralyzed prey. My mother sang to me
as she breastfed, chafed nipple

red as the egg from which I sprang.
Hours grew long, then longer. Late summer:

I wanted everything at once, an echo
forming from cries her body couldn't resist.

I'm here, she said, meaning my birth
like the overworked plot was planned.

Like the nectarine's recessive gene,
the wasp sings a predator's song

as defense. Cellulose breathes. The plant's
sex is freed. I will use the voice she gave me.

IV.

Past the Egg Room

Harvard Museum of Natural History

Past jarred millipedes and sea
lice, pale

      genitals, shriveled hide
tanned; past *African*

Giagantus (squatting like a Mayan
warrior buried
      facing east to bait back
the sun)—the amphibian's

      *

lower lip
      weighted, as if
by some invisible hook—the *Great*

      Hall of Birds
another taxidermied language
      altogether (its script

one everlasting gesture): un-
able to lament

      *

the sedge wrens, warblers,
swifts, nor loss of
      trees, the canopy goes
missing. Flight-

stripped fall, with its icy
                    words of alarm,
won't incite
the annual avian rites. Spring's

                    *

minor cues are left implied,
the breasts
                    stuffed with paper

strips of cedar. Thus, rooting
down migrates
                    inward—accounting
for the birds'

                    *

stiffening as they mimic ascension:
sharp clefts
                    of bones stretched

in air: the many thousands
pinned in
                    enduring ecstasy,

now-vacant skulls cocked back
to expose the feathers'

                    soft undercarriage of air-

                    *

brushed throats. What choice had they
in surrendering
                                    their debris

of song? What small

                    instrument scooped out
each fraction
                    of a single ounce
of heart?

                              *

I don't want this stuffed world,
but what's gone

                    missing: a glass box packed
with the birds'
                    meaty engines

that taken together
appear no more than a cluster
                                    of cells and blood,

                              *

the webbed lungs
loosed, or the trashed half-

                    foot of uncoiled intestine,

eyes which (if not freed
of their cords)

                              would tremble

*

in accusation—or strike us down
with their glazed

      look of recognition,

the fluid-filled lenses
welled up at last with cries

we'll no longer

      let them make.

This Way to the Egress

*I'd rather be a racehorse and last a minute, than a plow-horse and
last forever.*
          —Lillian Lietzel, aerialist, 1892–1931

Through the smoke-draped rafters, swinging

again and again, she's beating
her record: *333, 334*
          when the brass connection

    snaps—pitching her out

from the mottled spotlight
through the generators' ceaseless humming
into concussive darkness—

her greatest feat: plummeting four stories
to concrete, all 95 pounds of

The World's Most Marvelous Lady Gymnast

carried off in a stretcher. Shocked
at the neck-cord, spinal
shards tatter the protective
          net of her lungs. A hush
seizes the tent. Paler

by shadows of candle and crowd, she is briefly
stirred at the egress,
          acting as though
the view from below's no different,

as though she no longer cares

her father will charge a sixpence
to view his daughter's corpse.

To My Father Two Years into Death

At eight, I watched you chase a runaway
steer, the one that dared outwit you, the one

branded in scars on its side. Of course,
I wasn't there when you finally
faced it down, though I know too well

how suddenly you could turn. For years
I've wondered what I missed by falling

so far behind, so terrified of the steer,
and why I cling to the imagined moment
you fell, the moment there was so little

difference between you and it—the beast
blood-red and you, under it, bleeding.

I've gone back to that day, that hour
and stood, my frame filling the hole,
watched myself as a child, struggling.

But I'm left with only the image
of you: always more animal than man,

you watch yourself weep in the wet
glass of its tar-black eye, your darkened brow
cast down and defeated, your madness

broken in a chest of shattered ribs.
Father, because you are two years

and twenty-six days in the grave now,
it's safe to admit that though most daughters
would have cheered for their father,

I was pulling for the steer, and like the steer,
was always waiting.

The Hydra

Everything desirable is someplace else—
    even longing itself, disguised as a plant
        shop that readily stocks the ordinary
lilies, geraniums, mums, yet soon

    reveals, panting at the water's upper-
        most seam, an illegal, too-large-for-its-tank
Brazilian eel. Anchored by the white-mouthed,
    multi-faced electric tube: smaller eels
        knotting, un-knotting. It's Tuesday,

the street sweeper's steady hum rattles
    the fishes. Corals shift. A delicate, blue-
        spotted stingray glides by like a flattened bat,
submarine axis unaffected. At the aquarium
    you touched one; held a starfish,

    refused a slug. Your father once pulled
a ray up from the pier and released it
    into a white plastic bucket (or was it
        an ice-chest?). As it flopped on its slick, gray side,
you thought about asking him to let it go

    but, fixed on its movements, stood
        watching the spastic tail. Even then you'd heard
the myth of the hydra—tentacles thrashing,
    dividing into something unwanted—
        which wasn't the thick green eel, nor the ray

in your father's ice-chest, most certainly, not
    his wife—her wordlessness, her disheveled
        appearance, the astonished pleading from
her open mouth, moaning *ah but ah* but *oh.*

Pomegranate

Even now, I can see the seeded
apple between my mother's fingers—
full, heavy, persistent—and the tubular

calyx that guards the tart-sweet pith
inside. In her absence, I can feel
the care she took to split the hard

fruit open. Tracing the chamber
with my fingers, she likened the fruit
to my heart and the slow, sustaining

muscle that was her own thick heart.
Gently, as if it were a child struck
with fever, she held the pomegranate,

pulsing faintly throbbing against
my ear. Still it pleased her,
as it pleases me, to stain my tongue,

hands, and the white flesh that binds
each seed to the walls of its ruby
chamber. I break apart an *Early Foothill*.

July. The valley is hot, harvested—
strange, what a body withstands.
Stranger still this emptiness,

What now. Mother. What now?

Canopy

One of us flourished near running
      water; the other, born intolerant

          of shade. Years fasting, I'm split
      as a wishbone, still terrified
by the branches: the air: that dark

riot of song that passed like grief
      through the tangled aspens toward us.

          The rest, I'm afraid is true:
      our father never loved you—
No. Truth told, it was me

he never loved: too cold (he felt?)
      weak-minded. We've come

          once more to this wooded edge—
      spooked, you head for the clearing.
Brother, how can I make you

see? There was never any beast.
      No host of birds. It was he

          who rattled the canopy: the spattered
      trunk holding its ground
no matter how long, how hard—

night after night—the wind-
      beaten leaves cried out, to be let go

After Reading Chu Shu-Chen, I Cube a D'Anjou

All of the fruit trees—
                    cut back and disappearing.
          The world in
my parents' yard is
small and bare. As long as I am flesh
                    and bone,
the kingfishers mating near the streambed
will cause embarrassment.
                    I am tired of
          pinning up my hair.
The pear is not to blame.
The rain is not to blame.
          The grass pushes up
                              each blade
                    sharper than the next.
Into a pewter dish, I set
aside the piebald flesh,
                    its perfume
                    so spare—how long
will I sit at my father's table?

Here Hangeth His Death in the Yard

If seconds is what it takes to excavate the reared tarantula
If John Wayne is nowhere in sight
If the female spider is *solitary, velveteen, loathsome*
If *female* is always *a killer*

If disease of the heart is the commonest killer
If the commonest answer, *Amen*
If the girl, when prompted, kisses her father

If prompted from a series of slides to identify the human embryo,
    two out of three argue *goldfish*, yet a family of four can agree to name
    their pet goldfish *John Wayne*
If goldfish never remember
If embryos can't recall

If networks agree, a father's health can't be claimed, the root of familial
    disease can't be claimed, and no one—not one—has nerve enough
    to claim what he or she loves best

If loving best means claiming no one
If thou *thurstus* (see dryness, desire, terrain)
If Sunday's forecast calls *scattered showers*

If Sister Grète catches the girl ripping earthworms
    after the rainstorm in twos,
    orders her in from the playground for scolding
If misunderstanding, the girl admits she sneaks after school
    in the convent

If when guided into a room, handed a doll and told *show me*—
    the doll's little legs bow open:

oh, the Little Drummer Boy's bowlegged
the Scarecrow and Tin Woodman, bowlegged
see Jane skip through the park, bowlegged

If, northbound, a train transporting eight freights of goats (all bowlegged)
    passes through Hannover at precisely six-fifteen, holding up
    an ambulance en route to a five-car pile-up
If, in commiseration, one cries out

If the *whoosh* of the boxcar stifles this cry but lifts and deposits
    a fine silk hair that glistens and shines on the tracks,
    attracting a tired old crow
If crows are typically filthy birds

If the crow, over its lifetime, is a witness
    not to one, but three, six, eighty-eight gardens

If a man leads the girl past such-and-such garden
    to a gated pool where beneath the weeping hornbeam he undresses

If all the while whistling
    softly,
    he folds her nightdress
    into a neat little square:

        oh, the moon is an open eye
        (the moon never remembers)
        the child's eyes, too, are open
        (the embryo never sees)

If jutting the perimeter, he skims the wall's edge,
    swimming faster, faster,
        revving the underwater axel, until propelled by the current
        the girl and man move together and together and together

If diving wakes the water, and the girl's flesh, too
If those born late-June are Cancers,
          and what, but disease, is cancer?
If for father, the certificate indicates *Arie*

If falling one letter short of some higher constellation,
   Arie changes his name to *Bill*
If, approaching his fifty-first birthday, he falls twelve flights to his death
If the fallen man isn't her father
If the fallen man *wasn't* her father

If the fallen man weren't my father,
   what above remains fact?
If half, if a fourth, if a fraction
If truth's better third is invention
If ever daughter's a verb

Prometheus as Sparrow

Unstitched by the crow's ripper:
which part of us: beak gashing

the breast's tiny seam: *wants denial?*
attracted to: the bird will not

explode with: *what we think*:
its fragile note—whistle or trill:

we can get away with: the only
sound, a dull thump:

physical thing: as it is galled
against the sidewalk: *we cannot know*

by seeing: the young stalked above
learns too late to avoid: *or sense*

at looking: the risk of shiny things:
foil strip; chain unstrung; heat,

slick as the crow's silk cloak:
restraint does not: draped over

the life it will undo: *become us*:
mouth by cue a mechanical

instrument that scissors open:
he who sways: the meat it hangs

above: *will bend*: beak unloosing:
then break: the gray entrails, gutting

this body, self: *who needs*
denial, myth we live and die by

V.

Self-Portrait as (Super/Sub) Pacific

In the dark undersurface of sea,
        five hundred fathoms beneath,
dark as the giant squid's indigestible beak

lodged inside the sperm
        whale's second belly, the ocean's
sleek anatomy reveals itself:

in fossilized cuttlebone, dull clams,
        in the bloodbelly-comb jelly's
sorry remains—there, flashing

                *

their bacterial specks like sequins,
        slime eels entering (by
mouth, anus, by bloated gill) the dead

or dying. Attacked, their nerveless pink
        heads cock up, first puckered
then folded inward. Tell me,

which living thing can help
        but suffocate itself—when threatened,
what daughter won't work

                *

herself in knots? In another time,
        along an isolated strip, my father
leads me to a seaside cave. Outside, naked

bodies shine like rocks. With no more
          order than the washed-up
left-for-dead, rows of women

    bathing like ready brides, their
          nipples and hips faced up. Lying
on my back listening

                    *

    for the coming tide, I stack stones
          on my chest trying to attract
his attention, watching him

    watch what I can't
          understand—why he pushes me
in the cave at the sound

    of approaching footsteps. Since then,
          such thoughts have turned to
relics; I bury them in sand. From that cavern,

                    *

    which is no more than a fault
          in my mind, I've seen the sun—
some 90 million miles over the Pacific—

    dip down, as if to pierce the surface
          and somehow change it:
day after day, blue-

    black giving up its corals and pinks.
          Mother says the sea is a woman
tossing nature's greatest curves:

*

so barnacled white and blue, the she-
        whale shadows her newborn, cresting
every few seconds, for weeks refusing sleep

    to protect her calf. And the sand
        crab bears 40,000 eggs
on its back—what have I borne

    on mine? unable to pry my eyes
        from the dark green forms of those
who made me. On a calmer night;

*

    in gentler weather. When the bay of
        silence between them was still a harbor.
And the ship set sail. And from two

    thousand miles, the heart-
        shaped turtle returned to nest,
her hatchling's sex (unlike mine)

    determined by heat. At this point
        in a body that can carry
another to term, I've determined only

*

    the coldest mothers breed males.
        Still, I've made no great migration,
but battle the past for hours—knowing

no matter how calm it appears,
      the tide will soon be pulled beneath me.
Facing it, one sees smaller waves

    always give way to the greater—
      it was a man, my father so often told me,
whose words parted the sea. Looking out,

          *

I wonder how many pounds of marine
      snow drift each year from this
very surface, dusting miles of

    downed bone? Meanwhile, microscopic
      male tubers wriggle their barbed
heads into an egg sac (nights

    I've felt sex's similar current): un-
      witting host (half mother /
lover) grazing the marrow-rich

          *

bone-yards of whale. Fact: a baleen
      yields five tons of oil, sustaining
creatures by the hundreds; thus, from one carcass

    emerges an ecosystem
      that will thrive for a thousand years.
Fact: I, too, feed on debris

that will never surface—my thirst,
　　　an inherited thirst, like an infant's
appetite for milksong, which is sweet,

　　　　　*

　　but only half as sweet as the taste
　　　　of my brother's bones. As when
(in certain breeds of shark)

　　one stalks the uterine tank,
　　　　grazing on lesser embryos
stalled in the dark

　　chamber of their mother. Heart-
　　　　starved, the soon-
born will consume each womb-

　　　　　*

　　mate until it is, at last, alone.
　　　　But why blame one for wounding
what is nearest? Captive,

　　a nurse shark was found to have
　　　　in her stomach a human arm
so well preserved, the victim

　　recognized the milk-green cross-
　　　　bones tattooed across the wrist. Ankle
bone, drip-bag, the scarred half-

　　　　　*

moon stamped across his lip—which of
    my father's hard facts might be
softening inside me? If so, am I so

    unlike the osedax feeding off whale fall,
        working the meat-stripped carcass
at the bone? No eyes, legs, mouth—

    nothing to ferry me across the cold
        seeps and hydrothermal vents,
what choice have I but to devour

          *

    the discarded? *Osedax*—whose very name
        houses the sound of loss
in flux—hearing it, I can almost detect

    those plumes whose never-ending
        appetite means death: the male
(whose nature is to disguise itself,

    burrowing in) two bits parasite, two mate—yes,
        in death, such obscured selves
are, at last, released. Too late! Split

          *

    open, the host cannot know
        the hundred forms fled
from her side to colonize

another. Quick as a sea whip
      (which is neither quick, nor whole),
they disperse, absolved of the body

    that's held them. But who am I
      to question the world's design?
For good reason, the giant red mysid appears

          *

    black in the deep's dim-green.
      And the sea cucumber breathes
through its anal ring; in danger,

    sheds its organs, crawls away. In darkness,
      I, too, have found it easy parting with
the heart—swift and mercenary,

    divided from my body, some part
      bleats but cannot be heard, as sound
will change the pressure of its medium

          *

    when it moves. Like love being called
      regret, regret, or a father's sickness
(I cannot bring myself to say

    the word) which lodges itself
      in the gene pool. Lampfish, bristle-
mouth, predatory

tunicate—confined below, these know
       unceasing night, as blind
anglers cannot perceive light, but rather

      *

read the current. I have eyes,
       yet cannot see to say what it is
I am. Drifting through days'

    waves, crying (not), casting (not),
       stumbling among the rocks,
grasses, dunes, half-numb to

    the ocean's loathsome drone. Am I not
       half water? Crawling
so close to the bottom,

      *

do I not sing? I listen. I listen. The sets
       hurry to communicate. Cast red and green,
I have come to the edge

    they seem to say in the margins
       before breaking. I, too, have come,
carried from some great blue

    distance, only to find my buried
       self washed up tonight alongside
litter and rot. Among dust and weeds,

      *

beneath satellites that have for centuries
         guided men, I can barely make out
her figure. Is she stranded

    there on the periphery?
         No. Tonight, the bay's estuaries
offer up their smooth white swords—

    as if called, she crosses the dark
         green border, rising from the brine-
specked tide, gliding toward

                    *

    the shadow of her making. I listen.
         I listen—the water is full
of many shapes. A great fog

    pushes back the Pacific's
         restless hills. And the past rises
again before me. As I

    navigate its pitched surface
         daughter   lover   sister   other
no myth I was holds true.

Notes

In "Portrait *Hepialus*," details about the ghost moth are drawn from Richard Conniff's *Spineless Wonders*. The phrases "survive[s] on a diet of tears" and "flowerlike catkins" are borrowed from Conniff's chapter "Ghosts on Wings."

"Two-Headed Nightingale" is the stage name of conjoined songstresses Christine and Millie McCoy. Born into slavery, the sisters were attached at the lower spine, sold to a showman early in their lives and kidnapped several times. They sang and danced to rave reviews both in the United States and overseas, and could speak five languages. As is often the case with twins whose bodies were joined in utero, after Millie died of tuberculosis in 1912, Christine soon followed.

"Automata" is indebted to *The Bloody Chamber: And Other Stories* by Angela Carter.

"Recovery by Anonymous, c. 1950," the apple wood sculpture featured in "Song for the Catatonic," is housed at Baltimore's American Visionary Art Museum. Some liberties have been taken with the artist's biography.

"Genealogical Survey across Several Counties" is inspired by Terrance Hayes's "The Blue Terrance" ("I come from a long line hollowed out on a dry night...") published in *Wind in a Box*.

In "Hopkins at the Window," facts and excerpts from the poet's letters are culled from Paul Mariani's biography *Gerard Manley Hopkins: A Life*.

"Past the Egg Room" is for Michael Tomola.

photo by K. Templeton

Shara Lessley is a former Wallace Stegner Fellow in Poetry at
Stanford University. Her awards include an Artist Fellowship
from the State of North Carolina, the Diane Middlebrook Poetry
Fellowship from the Wisconsin Institute for Creative Writing, an
Olive B. O'Connor Fellowship from Colgate University, The
Gilman School's Tickner Fellowship, and a "Discovery"/*The
Nation* prize. Shara's poems have appeared in *Ploughshares*, *The
Kenyon Review*, *The Southern Review*, and *The Missouri Review*,
among others. She currently lives in Amman, Jordan.

The New Issues Poetry Prize

Andrew Allport, *the body | of space | in the shape of the human*
2011 Judge: David Wojahn

Jeff Hoffman, *Journal of American Foreign Policy*
2010 Judge: Linda Gregerson

Judy Halebsky, *Sky=Empty*
2009 Judge: Marvin Bell

Justin Marks, *A Million in Prizes*
2008 Judge: Carl Phillips

Sandra Beasley, *Theories of Falling*
2007 Judge: Marie Howe

Jason Bredle, *Standing in Line for the Beast*
2006 Judge: Barbara Hamby

Katie Peterson, *This One Tree*
2005 Judge: William Olsen

Kevin Boyle, *A Home for Wayward Girls*
2004 Judge: Rodney Jones

Matthew Thorburn, *Subject to Change*
2003 Judge: Brenda Hillman

Paul Guest, *The Resurrection of the Body and the Ruin of the World*
2002 Judge: Campbell McGrath

Sarah Mangold, *Household Mechanics*
2001 Judge: C.D. Wright

Elizabeth Powell, *The Republic of Self*
2000 Judge: C.K. Williams

Joy Manesiotis, *They Sing to Her Bones*
1999 Judge: Marianne Boruch

Malena Mörling, *Ocean Avenue*
1998 Judge: Philip Levine

Marsha de la O, *Black Hope*
1997 Judge: Chase Twichell